Campaign Branding
Building a Political Reputation

by Michael McNamara

CAMPAIGNGUY
★ ★ ★ ★ ★ PRESS

Published by Campaignguy Press,
an imprint of Mason Grant, LLC
West Chester, Ohio
Campaignguy Press, and the "Campaignguy" logo are
trademarks of Mason Grant, LLC

ISBN: 978-1-944266-11-0

CONTENTS

Introduction

With over two decades of advising hundreds of successful campaigns for office, I have experienced every type of race. From local liquor options and precinct representatives for a local political party all the way to Congressional and U.S. Senatorial races, I have seen it all. Candidates who have sought my help range from teenagers to seniors, millionaires and penniless single parents. My clients through the years range a large spectrum of diverse individuals and organizations.

One thing almost every client has in common is a lack of understanding about their campaign brand and why it is important to their campaign plan and winning.

Many candidates think that a campaign brand is the logo they place on a yard sign. As you will learn in this short publication, a brand is so much more than just a yard sign.

Winning a campaign is also much more than a brand, but these pages will get you started on your way to developing a strong brand for your campaign. To learn more about building an effective campaign, how to fundraise, developing a message, and how to successfully deliver that message, please read *The Political Campaign Desk Reference* available on Amazon and other bookstores.

If you are reading this short book about campaign branding, I can easily assume that you are interested in winning a campaign. If so, please finish reading and then pick p a copy of *The Political Campaign Desk Reference*. You will not be disappointed. *The Political Campaign Desk Reference* will walk you through the process of applying what you learn in Campaign Branding and integrating your brand into your campaign. *The Political Campaign Desk Reference* will provide you with ideas for fundraising and help walk you through that process including tools such as sample fundraising letters and scripts for when you are making those important calls to potential donors.

But before you start all that, you need to understand your brand and develop your brand. Your brand is more than your logo. Your brand is your story. It is what people think about you when they hear your name, see your yard sign, or read about you.

Early in my consulting career, I sat down with a candidate who was older and had successfully run his own business for decades. He was near retirement age and wanted to pass his business along to his children as he pursued public service. When I began to discuss the importance of building a brand, he stopped me.

"Son," he said. "I'm just talking to you because everyone told me that I had to if I wanted to win. I'm not interested in all this 'branding' baloney. I built my business from nothing when I got out of the service. I did it through hard work, and that's how I'm going to do it now. So what can you tell me that's going to help me win?"

I asked this prospective client a few pointed questions about himself and his business. In just a few minutes, his attitude took an about-face, and by the end of our lunch he was a believer. He did everything I recommended and won his race against an opponent who had spent more than we did.

Another candidate that I met also stopped me when I first began our discussion about branding. She had hired a graphic designer and explained that she already had a brand that she loved. She pulled out some sheets of paper with various logos that looked like they could be perfect for a hair salon or fancy coffee shop that might close after a couple of years. She thought she would appear glamorous because of the fancy, curly fonts. The logos were also over-messaged with too much wording and information. She had broken every rule for creating a logo. White noise would have been more pleasant. It took her a couple of weeks to finally let go of her preconceived notions and logos. She was devastated that she could not use them (at least if she wanted to win). She followed my advice, kept her image simple and clean, and she won.

In the first case, my client thought that blunt force would win the day. He felt that by being a hard worker that his opponents would not keep up. He did not think that creating a brand and image would allow him to make more effective and efficient use of his time, money and energy. He was able to keep an open mind in our initial meeting, and he won.

In the second case, my client left our meeting having decided not to hire me. She felt that I had insulted her efforts. All I did was ask her a few questions to help her come to the self-realization that she needed a makeover. I was nothing but complimentary. She later understood that the conclusions that we came to during our meeting were hers based on her own answers to my questions. After she accepted the fact that her logos had nothing to do with winning a campaign, she contacted me and hired me. She won. We remain good friends to this day.

As you learn about branding in this short manual, understand that it is merely one small aspect of a larger campaign plan. If you feel the information here is useful, then please learn more by checking out *The Political Campaign Desk Reference* and learn how to incorporate branding into your comprehensive campaign plan.

My final disclaimer is that the advice in this short publication is relevant for a vast majority of political campaigns. There are campaigns, however, that have parochial characteristics that may seem to invalidate the general advice found here. This uniqueness is why it is important for candidates who are serious about winning to hire a professional who can understand the unique local characteristics of a race and to pivot where necessary on general advice.

Thank you for reading this publication. Best wishes for a successful campaign!

What is branding all about?

When someone thinks of a brand, they tend to immediately conjure images of logos from recognizable companies. They might equate a brand with an image or even a slogan or tag line. Some might feel that a brand is the service or good that a company or person provides.

A brand is so much more than a logo, a slogan, or knowing what services or goods someone offers.

A brand is how people feel about your products. It is an understanding of the quality of your service or goods. You brand is what people say about you even if they have never met you. Your brand is how people feel when they see your yard signs. Your brand is the essence of everything that someone might think about when they come in contact with your image, your name, or anything associated with you.

A public servant will spend their entire career developing and building their brand. Everything that a politician says or does from the moment they enter public life has the potential of becoming part of that person's brand. How they vote on legislation, how they treat others, and their political philosophy becomes part of their story that will be repeated by others. Brilliant comments as well as gaffes are part of the brand.

A yard sign and a slogan are mere manifestations of how the candidate chooses to promote their brand.

When I sit down with a prospective client, I generally make it an opportunity to listen. I want to understand what that candidate's self-image is and what they believe is their reputation. I will ask various questions that help the candidate come to a self-realization that selecting the image for their race is vital to their success.

Some of the questions I ask might include:
- What do you think a brand is?
- What do you think YOUR brand is?
- So you think you have a killer logo. That's great. What do people think about when they see your logo on yard signs and other materials?
- What story are you trying to tell during your campaign?
- Is that story told in your logo, or is your logo the focal point that will help people remember your story once they've heard it?

- How does your logo help tell your story?
- Will people instantly understand you and your candidacy if they look at your logo?

Once we get through these basic questions and have an honest discussion about their self-image, we enter a bigger conversation about what they want to accomplish on their campaign. You see, some candidates run for office the first time not to win – sometimes they run because they are trying to build a reputation and image to position themselves for an attempt at another office. They run for a more local office to build a base of support with voters. The risk, of course, is building the wrong reputation which may undermine a run for a different office.

Branding is about your story. It is the story that you are telling the voters. It is the reputation that you want during your entire political career.

So if you are a candidate reading this, think about this question: should you be more concerned about your logo and your slogan or how people think about you when they see your images?

A comprehensive campaign plan is a plan that is designed to build your brand. It is not a document that is molded around an image that a graphic designer created for you. Your brand is not the colors you use. And it is not the slogan on your materials. All these elements are important in illustrating your brand. However, your brand is more valuable than any words on a sign. It is your essence, and it is what people will use to make judgments about you and whether to vote for you or not.

Therefore, it is important to create a brand that is simple. Older candidates may have myriad experiences that they want all voters to know. They want voters to know all the jobs they have held, their positions on all issues, their life story, their relatives, and what awards they received in high school. When voters are making decisions, they are not going to pay attention to political noise. Voters want a few simple things as they choose how to vote:

1) What you will do for them
2) How you will do it better, faster, and cheaper than the other person
3) Your relevant experience
4) Military service
5) Your party affiliation

I have had candidates argue with me that it is important to remind voters how they were the winning quarterback on the football team 30 years before. Other candidates wanted to create an "issues" page on their web site for a local office that took a position on issues that had no relation to the position being sought.

Your brand should revolve around your ability to get the job you are seeking accomplished. Your brand should resonate with voters as a brand that gets things done and does them well.

So when you build your brand in the next section, remember to keep it simple, and keep it relevant.

So how do I start this whole branding thing?

Remember in Chapter 1 that we discussed what voters want to know most about a candidate. Based on over a quarter of a century of running campaigns, I have found that voters do not have the capacity to know, weigh, and understand the details of the lives of all the candidates for all the races in each election cycle. I have not met anyone who has that capacity. Understanding that the human brain processes billions of bits of information daily, you must be able to penetrate a voter's attention. To do that, your brand must speak to what they care about most.

The five things that voters typically care about when selecting a candidate are:

1) What you will do for them
2) How you will do it better, faster, and cheaper than the other person
3) Your relevant experience
4) Military service
5) Your party affiliation

What will you do for them?

When developing your brand, you want voters to understand that you will accomplish what they want. Is it to lower taxes? Is it to promote job growth? Is it to address crime? Or is it to improve the quality of life? There is a process to determine what voters care about. This process is mapped out in *The Political Campaign Desk Reference*. The purpose of this publication is to guide you to making the issue that voters care about part of your brand.

If voters are concerned about lower taxes, do you think that your position on greenhouse gases is going to be important to them? This doesn't mean that you have to give up your passion about the environment, but it does mean that you should be disciplined enough to understand your audience and accentuate the portion of your platform that will penetrate. Remember that you are competing with billions of bits of information that each voter processes, and if you don't talk about what they care about, then you have lost an opportunity to develop a strong brand.

Remember to keep it simple. A common mistake for candidates is to develop a web page and direct mail materials that discuss all the platform positions the candidate holds. No person can process and remember all the positions any one candidate can hold. In fact, I have seen candidates undermine themselves because they say something on the public record that contradicts their stated position on their web site.

Instead of trying to take a position on everything, it is often more effective to take the one position that voters care most about and make that singular issue your brand. Own the issue. Stake out your position on that issue that resonates with voters, and become the political embodiment of the issue. Be the solution people are looking for. Do not distract yourself and dilute your brand by staking out a position on every national issue. Select the local issue most important to your audience.

One thing I have seen done successfully is for a campaign to have volunteers contact an opponent's campaign and ask them where they stand on a plethora of issues. If the opponent feels compelled to begin staking a position on dozens of issues, then they are beginning to dilute their brand, and they begin losing ground to my candidate. Of course, it is important for a candidate to stay focused and disciplined on their own campaign. If one of my candidates begins to receive a large number of contacts requesting positions on various issues that do not even have anything to do with our brand, I will simply direct those people to our web site for more information and inform them that we are focused on the issue(s) we have defined for this race.

The things to remember are:
- Keep it simple
- Keep your number of issues minimal
- Stay disciplined on your issue and own the issue for that campaign cycle

How will you do it better, faster, and cheaper than the other person?

If you are going to own an issue, you must stake out the correct position on that issue. Does that mean you have to compromise your values? No. It means that your position should be authentic to you and intersect an issue that voters care about. If the position is authentic to you, then you will be more comfortable and believable when you articulate how you will do it better, faster, and cheaper than the opponent.

Remember that you must keep it simple to explain and simple to understand. If you are unable to express your position on an issue in a few words and a couple of photos, then maybe you should select another relevant issue. Remember that you are still competing with billions of bits of information bombarding your audience each day. If you are fortunate enough to gain a voter's attention, you will likely only have it for a very brief period – a matter of seconds. You must be compelling and brief in your position and convince your audience that you are better equipped to successfully manage the issue that voters care about.

A mistake that many inexperienced candidates make is not following through with their message and expressing how they will work for voters better than their opponent. Candidates often have an unfounded fear that drawing a contrast is "going negative" and therefore dirty and underhanded. Think of it this way: when you are making a big money purchase, you likely compare brands, read reviews, and try to make the best decision about the products you are buying. Voters do the same thing, but voters do not often seek out information on their own when selecting which candidate to choose. Voters need to know which candidate will work for them in a better way than the other. If the campaigns are not expressing their strengths, and exposing their opponent's weaknesses, effectively, then voters will have to make a decision on other points such as military service or party affiliation. Be the candidate whose branding includes why they are best suited for the job and do not be afraid to draw a contrast.

It sounds easy, but finding the right mix of words, the most compelling images, making it brief, keeping it relevant, staying disciplined on the issue, and being articulate is a challenge. I have seen political consultants who have been running campaigns for years still be unable to master the development of a message that helps to define a brand.

Your relevant experience

If your position is to defend the Second Amendment, is it important to tell voters what high school you attended? If you want to fix a crime problem, should you spend your resources telling voters what your religion is?

Your biography is part of your brand. Although many people may read a thousand-page biography on George Washington, those people are not going to read more than a couple of paragraphs of the biography of a candidate for a local office. Remember that you are competing against billions of bits of information being processed by voters. You are lucky if you get one of them to notice you. You are even luckier if you get them to understand your issue for the campaign. It is even more rare for a voter to spend any time reading your biography. If you have an audience who is looking at your biography, do you think it is more important to weave a narrative over many lengthy, burdensome and intimidating paragraphs, or should you select the top three components of your background and make them bullet points?

Hint: go with the three (no more than three) bullet points.

The only people who will read a lengthy "'Issues" page and extensive "Biography" page are people who want you to hire them and your opponent's campaign. The former group wants to find out how to connect with you so you will purchase their services, and the other is trying to exploit anything they can find in your background. The more information you make available, the more vulnerable you make yourself to both groups.

Pick the top background point and make that your story. If you are running to be Solicitor or Prosecutor or District Attorney, then maybe your one biographical point is the most heinous criminal you put behind bars. A singular case can turn into a story that illustrates in pictures and a few words how you are tough on crime, how you put the bad guys behind bars, and how you have the right experience.

Don't talk about your family. Don't talk about your grade school or high school. Talk about the one thing you did that made a difference in the lives of others. Talk about the life you saved or the criminal you prosecuted. Talk about how you fought a tax increase. Talk about your activism on an issue. Whatever it is, just pick one relevant biographical point and build that into your message and your brand.

Military service

Military service is an important biographical detail that is typically important to communicate. A candidate who has a military background likely has images of being in uniform, possibly taking an oath, or being in a unit of diverse individuals who are protecting their country. With a single word or image denoting military service, an entire story can be told. The story is one of sacrifice and contributing to the greater good. The story includes service and selflessness.

Candidates with military experience should always communicate their prior service in their campaigns. There is a fine line, however, of making military service an important point to making it the only focus of a candidate. If military service were the only powerful message, then John McCain would have defeated Barack Obama, and Bob Dole would have defeated Bill Clinton. Candidates must still communicate what they will do for voters and how they will do it better.

Military service can be an important detail, but it must be effectively integrated into the brand and not be the brand.

Party affiliation

Some areas of the United States are very polarized. There are Congressional and state legislative districts that have been created to favor a specific party. In these districts, party affiliation may be the only branding point that a candidate needs to win. This fact can be frustrating for a challenger from the minority party in a district.

In more competitive districts, however, a candidate's political party may not appeal to all voters. Communicating the political affiliation of a candidate can still be useful to a brand in a competitive district, but the use of political affiliation should be targeted to voters who will respond favorably. Effective targeting is discussed in more detail in the book *The Political Campaign Desk Reference*.

There are some voters who fail to research candidates and their positions. However, these people still vote. When they make their decision for whom to vote, they may follow the slate card of a political party. The slate card will list all that party's endorsed candidates for each position on the ballot. Slate cards targeted to the homes of loyal party voters can be powerful when a candidate needs to achieve support.

Be judicious on the use of party affiliation. It is still most important to make your brand about what you will do and how you will do it better.

Conclusion

As you develop your brand, think about what issues are most

important to voters. Are voters concerned about whether you graduated from a local high school, or are they more worried about whether they will have a job next year? Are they motivated by what you accomplished as a teenager at your first job, or are they more interested in how your education, experience and training will lead to a more successful, safer environment if you are elected?

Your brand should be forward-thinking. Do not dwell on the past. When voters make decisions, they are thinking more about how you will benefit them and less about what you did in college or high school. Although your past accomplishments might help tell the story about how you are capable of being successful in the next term in office, you must first present a clear case that you understand the issues about which voters care.

What Does My Brand Look Like?

I have participated in hundreds of campaigns and races over decades in politics. Many of the candidates with whom I have worked agonized over the specific colors they would use in their logo. Some have read articles they found online while others tried to incorporate the local school district's colors. Candidates have also agonized over the font they would use. Other considerations that candidates consider include whether to include a slogan, their party, the office they are seeking, and clip art type devices.

The worst logos and signs I have ever seen try to include all these facets, and they turn out to be political nonsense when they do. Undisciplined campaigns try to create a world-class logo and end up with a junkyard sculpture.

A campaign's brand should be, above all else, simple. For something to be memorable, it must be simple. For something to penetrate the attention of voters whose brains process billions of bits of information daily, the brand must be simple.

One of my favorite campaign logos that I show to audiences of all ages is the logo used by Dwight Eisenhower to run for President in 1952. The "I Like Ike" logo became iconic. Three words is all it was. They were placed on a round button divided into three colors – red, white and blue. It was easily transferable to a black-and white medium. And the logo became so powerful that the words "I" and "Like" were dropped from many versions, and the logo just read "Ike".

Local races are not national political campaigns, but they should follow the same rules when developing a brand and look. Think about your favorite college and how it might be branded with a single letter. That is powerful, but it is so simple. Think about politicians who you know simply by their initials: JFK, LBJ, W.

The key to winning a campaign is not about what colors you decide to use or what slogan you have. The key to using your brand effectively is simplicity and consistency.

Our most recognizable consumer brands will spend millions of dollars over years or decades to develop brand awareness and a solid reputation. Political campaigns are forced to develop brand awareness and reputation with a minute fraction of the budget in a very short amount of time – usually weeks or months instead of years and decades.

When I help a campaign develop the visual representation of its brand, I insist on a few important points:

The most prominent feature must be the candidate's name as this is how the voter will see the candidate on the ballot

- We are not President Eisenhower, so use the ballot name and not a nickname
- We can add the office for which we are running or the campaign message, but not both
- I typically do not have much input when it comes to color selection
- Once we settle on a campaign logo and colors, we do not use any other logo or color combination

When using a candidate's name, I typically only use the last name. Occasionally, I will add a candidate's first name on the logo if there is some significant reason.   Most commonly, I will add a female candidate's first name in a logo if we have evidence that voters will favor a candidate due to gender. I will also add either the office being sought or a campaign slogan that speaks to the candidate's brand and message, but I won't add both.

Each word you add to a political sign adds to its noise factor.   The noise factor is the addition of bits of information that causes the brain to process even more information before your brand can penetrate. Therefore, your own logo can work against you if you add too many words. Remember that the average human brain processes billions of bits of information each day. To penetrate, you need to keep the image of your logo simple. If you want your sign to be read, make it readable by eliminating as many words as possible.

This brings us to the discussion on font choice.   Bold, clear fonts without serifs follow the "keep it simple" rule. The fancier the font, the greater the noise factor. You can reduce your own noise by choosing an easy-to-read font.

Colors become a factor if they detract from your brand.   For instance, white letters on a yellow background are less readable. I like to choose background colors that contrast with lettering colors. White letters on a dark background work very well and stand out in the mail, in print, on signs and in electronic and broadcast ads.

When you build your brand, keep these simple points in mind, and you will be guided well:

1) Keep words to a minimum – eliminate ALL nonessential verbiage
2) Keep the font clean and simple – the fancier, the noisier
3) Choose colors that contrast with the colors of your words so your audience can read your message

Despite my experience that exceeds 25 years in political campaigns, my candidates will still argue with me on each of these points when developing a logo. They want to include a slogan and an office. They want to use first names as well. Some want to add a maiden name or middle name because they think that voters will recognize the name. Noise. Noise. Noise.

Do not take my word for it – look at the world's most recognizable corporate brands that have stood the test of time. Each of these brands follows the rules in this publication. The brand is simple, has few words, and it is easy to see. Why argue with a time-tested, successful approach that very smart people have developed? Candidates still argue with me, though, on these basic points.

How do I promote my brand?

There are myriad ways to promote your brand. To promote your brand correctly, it requires a comprehensive plan. I have spent my entire political career creating plans and refining the art of planning a political campaign. I outline the basics of campaign planning in my book *The Political Campaign Desk Reference.*

Since I started running political campaigns, I have heard people who dislike yard signs say, "yard signs don't vote." Sure. Neither does direct mail or television or electronic media. The best I can figure is that someone who did not want candidates buying yard signs came up with that saying as their "microphone drop" argument against signs. It is hard to argue against a statement like "signs don't vote" because they, in fact, do not vote; but that has nothing to do with how signs can be effective in marketing.

Among political consultants, there is great debate about whether spending money on political yard signs is worthwhile or not. Consultants who specialize in buying media often counsel that money must be spent on media. Direct mail specialists often counsel that direct mail is where money goes. But keep in mind that these consultants make money on the medium of their expertise.

I personally like to use signs on a campaign. They are relatively inexpensive, and they raise awareness of a campaign. According to PCSigns.com, where I have sourced my signs almost exclusively for nearly two decades, you can place a single road sign on a high traffic route for less than $50 and raise instant awareness of your campaign among hundreds or thousands of voters. Multiply that by dozens of road signs for major routes and a few hundred small signs for neighborhoods, and you have an effective method of starting your campaign.

Keep in mind that signs are only a start. Awareness is only one portion of a successful campaign. A successful campaign will integrate a web site, social media and other methods into its plan.

But the most important component of promoting your brand is consistency.

I have witnessed dozens of candidates who want to alter their campaign logo colors to each of the local school's colors for their signs and direct mail. This type of decision is a destructive choice that I refer to as dilution. By changing your logo's visual appearance from town-to-town forces you are diluting your own brand. This means that you have started to spend money to work against yourself.

Wherever your brand is used, it must be used consistently. The colors, fonts, message, and proportions should always remain the same once you have chosen them. Each time you change a component of your logo, you are creating a new brand that voters have never seen. Always be consistent.

The Political Campaign Desk Reference provides details on how to promote your message consistently and effectively through various media such as television, digital, direct mail, print, signs and more.

When promoting your brand, remember these important points:

- Always be consistent.
- Always have a plan.
- The entire campaign should never consist of using a single medium to promote awareness and advocacy.

Conclusion

When someone decides to run for political office, they often do not know where to begin. What they do know is that they want to get involved, or they want to change something, or politics interests them. Whatever the reason, there are many things to think about, and this short guide only touches upon a few of them.

I wrote this small publication to provide some food for thought for new candidates and those of you who have never run campaigns before. By no means should this advice be considered comprehensive. Many campaigns need a starting point, and that is what I attempt here. I wrote the first edition of *The Political Campaign Desk Reference* in 2008 and have constantly updated its editions. Although many campaigns are working to pinch pennies, I always recommend that a candidate who wants to win should hire an experienced, knowledgeable consultant.

Politics is a journey, and it can be enriching and fulfilling. It is difficult, however. Campaigns are about marketing ideas and people. Governing, making decisions, balancing budgets, listening to competing needs and ideas is something completely different, and few things adequately prepare candidates for their first day in office.

Work hard and meet as many people as you can. Above all else, the best candidates are listeners. Many candidates think that voters want someone in office who has all the answers. No one has all the answers. But if voters understand that they have a voice with you and that you will listen, then you are way ahead of your opponent already.

Your brand is your reputation and your story. Your brand is what people think about you. It is not your logo or your yard sign. The logo you develop is simply a representation of your brand. Your brand is what you will do for people and why you are the best candidate to do it.

Just remember a few simple rules when developing your brand:
- Keep it simple.
- Keep your message short.
- Tell the relevant parts of your story.
- Talk about what people care about.
- Be consistent.
- Have a plan.

And if you need to develop your campaign plan, then please get a copy of *The Political Campaign Desk Reference.*

17

ABOUT THE AUTHOR

Michael McNamara has been professionally consulting on campaigns at all levels for over 25 years. From nonpartisan issue campaigns and local liquor options to federal races for United States Congress and United States Senate, McNamara's experience is broad and deep when it comes to winning political campaigns.

McNamara graduated from Miami University in Oxford, Ohio and earned his Master of Public Administration from the Voinovich School of Leadership and Public Affairs at Ohio University in Athens, Ohio. McNamara has been a member of many professional organizations including the American Association of Political Consultants and the American Political Science Association.

McNamara resides in Ohio with his wife, Lisa, where they raise their two sons.

www.ingramcontent.com/pod-product-compliance
Lightning Source LLC
Chambersburg PA
CBHW071348290326
41933CB00041B/3146